WASPS AND BEES

BY MARIE PEARSON

The Child's World®
childsworld.com

Published by The Child's World®
1980 Lookout Drive • Mankato, MN 56003-1705
800-599-READ • www.childsworld.com

Photographs ©: Shutterstock Images, cover (wasp), cover (bee), 2, 3, 5, 10, 11, 13, 14, 15, 17, 20, 21, 24 (wasp), 24 (bee); Luc Pouliot/Shutterstock Images, 6; Rainer Fuhrmann/Shutterstock Images, 9; Jaco Visser/Shutterstock Images, 19

Copyright © 2020 by The Child's World®
All rights reserved. No part of this book may be reproduced or utilized in any form or by any means without written permission from the publisher.

ISBN 9781503835948
LCCN 2019943067

Printed in the United States of America

ABOUT THE AUTHOR

Marie Pearson is a children's book author and editor. She especially loves learning about animals and nature.

TABLE OF CONTENTS

CHAPTER 1 **Bugs That Sting**   4

CHAPTER 2 **Wasps**   7

CHAPTER 3 **Bees**   12

CHAPTER 4 **What's the Difference?**   18

Glossary   22
To Learn More   23
Activity   23
Index   24

CHAPTER 1

Bugs That Sting

A bug buzzes by. It is yellow and black. It has six legs. **Antennae** stick out of its head. Four wings beat quickly. Is it a bee or a wasp? How are they different?

A bee drinks nectar from a flower.

Wasps help gardens by hunting harmful insects.

CHAPTER
2

Wasps

Many wasps are black with shades of yellow or orange. They have a few hairs. Their bodies are long and thin. This helps them fly quickly.

Some female wasps have stingers. They sting to protect themselves. The stingers are smooth. They have **venom**. Wasps can sting many times.

Some adult wasps eat **nectar**. They also eat fruit juice. Many wasps look for food in trash bins at parks. Wasp **larvae** eat bugs and spiders. Adults hunt for the bugs.

Wasps' waists are narrow. This helps them move their stinger. They can use it to kill **prey**.

Some wasps eat food left by humans such as meat, fruit, or sugary drinks.

9

Some wasps make paper-like nests.

10

Some wasps live alone. They have nests in the ground. Others live in groups. They build nests in trees or on buildings. The nests are made of wood or plant stems. Wasps chew the wood and stems and spit them out. This makes them like paper.

CHAPTER 3

Bees

Bees are black with shades of yellow. They can have lots of hairs. The hairs make them look fuzzy. **Pollen** sticks to the hairs. Bees' bodies are rounded.

Bees carry pollen from plant to plant. Many plants use this pollen to make seeds.

Some people raise bees and harvest their honey.

Some female bees can protect themselves. They sting if they are threatened. Their stingers have hooks at the end. They get stuck in skin. Bees can only sting once. Then they die.

Bees get food from flowers. They eat pollen and nectar. They make some nectar into honey. Bees use honey as food for the whole **hive**. Bee larvae also eat nectar and honey.

Bees that live alone have nests in the ground. But some live in groups. They make a hive in a safe area, like a hole in a tree. The bees' bodies make wax. They use the wax to make the hive.

Some bees make waxy hives.

CHAPTER 4

What's the Difference?

Wasps are thin and sleek. Bees are round and fuzzy. Wasps can sting many times. Bees sting only once. Adult bees and larvae eat honey and nectar from flowers. Wasps eat nectar, too. But wasp larvae eat bugs. Wasp nests are like paper. Beehives are waxy.

Some bees, such as the cuckoo bee, look more like wasps.

Bees and wasps are sometimes not that different. Some bees look sleek like wasps. Some wasps' stingers get stuck in skin. Bees **evolved** from wasps. But they are all helpful bugs!

WASPS

Few hairs

Smooth stinger

Long, thin body

- Eat nectar and fruit juice
- Larvae eat bugs
- Build nests in the ground or paper-like nests

BEES

- Fuzzy
- Rounded body
- Hooks on stinger

- Eat pollen, nectar, and honey
- Larvae eat the same food as adults
- Build nests in the ground or waxy beehives

GLOSSARY

antennae (an-TEN-ee) Antennae are feelers on insects' heads. Both wasps and bees have antennae.

evolved (i-VAHLVD) Something that has evolved has changed slowly over time. Bees evolved from wasps.

hive (HYV) A hive is a waxy home that groups of bees make. Bees build a hive in a safe place.

larvae (LAHR-vuh) Larvae are the young, wormlike forms of certain animals that often don't look much like their adult forms. Wasp larvae eat bugs and spiders.

nectar (NEK-tur) Nectar is a sweet liquid inside flowers. Bees make some nectar into honey.

pollen (PAH-luhn) Pollen is the small, yellow grains on flowers that needs to be spread to other flowers so that the flowers can reproduce. Bees eat pollen and spread it from one flower to another.

prey (PRAY) Prey are animals that are eaten by other animals. Wasps sting their prey.

venom (VEN-uhm) Venom is a poison that gets injected into the body. Stingers shoot venom.

TO LEARN MORE

IN THE LIBRARY

Patterson, Jack K. *Wasps*. New York, NY: Cavendish Square, 2019.

Schnell, Lisa K. *Bees Buzz*. Vero Beach, FL: Rourke Educational Media, 2019.

Unstead, Sue. *Amazing Bees*. New York, NY: DK Publishing, 2016.

ON THE WEB

Visit our website for links about wasps and bees:
childsworld.com/links

Note to Parents, Teachers, and Librarians: We routinely verify our Web links to make sure they are safe and active sites. So encourage your readers to check them out!

ACTIVITY

Draw a picture of a wasp and a bee. Your picture should clearly show the differences between the wasp and the bee. Look at pages 20 and 21 for help.

INDEX

antennae, 4

body shape, 7–8, 12, 18

food, 8, 15

hair, 7, 12
hive, 15–16, 18
honey, 15, 18

larvae, 8, 15, 18

nectar, 8, 15, 18
nest, 11, 16, 18

pollen, 12, 15
prey, 8

stinger, 7–8, 14, 19

venom, 7